INSIDE THE HOOPS
A UNIQUE INSIGHT INTO CELTIC FOOTBALL CLUB

INSIDE THE HOOPS
A UNIQUE INSIGHT INTO CELTIC FOOTBALL CLUB

An official Celtic Football Club Publication	Concept Design and Print	With Thanks	Photography
First Published in Great Britain by	CRE8 (UK) Limited	Jules McGeever	Paul Broadrick
Celtic Football Club	The Old Brewery	Paul Cuddihy	Tony Hamilton
Celtic Park	Priory Lane	Joe Sullivan	Roman Michnowicz
Glasgow	Burford	Kenny MacLeod	
G40 3RE	OX18 4SG		

Copyright © 2006 Cre8 (UK) Limited

All rights reserved. No part of this publication may be reproduced, stored in a retrieval system, or transmitted in any form or by any means, electronic, mechanical, photocopying, recording or otherwise, without the prior permission of the copyright owner and the publishers.

CONTENTS
INSIDE **THE HOOPS**

007	INTRODUCTION	046	THE PLAYERS	114	THE MATCH
008	OUR PARADISE	070	THE PREPARATION	146	THE GAFFER
024	THE FANS	092	THE BUILD UP	160	CELTIC PEOPLE

INTRODUCTION

CELTIC Football Club is a world-famous sporting institution. The origins of the club's formation are unique in football and we remain proud of that fact, staying true to the ethos of Brother Walfrid through the excellent work of our Charity Fund.

We believe, as supporters, that Celtic is more than just a football club and to follow the team is to be part of a family that extends all over the world. We enjoy the triumphs and endure the disappointments, but our devotion to the Celtic cause remains undiminished. It is why, in song, we declare ourselves to be 'faithful through and through'.

The focal point for supporters has always been the players on the park, the men who, through their footballing ability, have been lucky enough to wear the famous green and white hoops. That is as it should be and will always remain the case. We are a football club and are judged on our success in the competitions we participate in.

What this book, Inside the Hoops, offers supporters, however, is a unique insight into Celtic Football Club, looking beyond what happens on the pitch during a match. The photographs capture what goes on behind the scenes at the club and allows supporters a glimpse of the inner workings of the club

From the training ground to the changing rooms, from supporters to the unsung heroes at Celtic Park, this publication chronicles the club as never seen before and I am sure every Celtic supporter will enjoy this rare opportunity to view these iconic images.

Brian Quinn
Chairman
Celtic Football Club

OUR PARADISE

LIKE THE PHOENIX RISING FROM THE ASHES, CELTIC PARK AROSE AMID THE EAST END OF GLASGOW AS A BEACON FOR FOLLOWERS OF THE CLUB THE WORLD OVER AND NO MATTER WHERE YOU GO IN THE WORLD THERE'S SOME CORNER OF A FOREIGN FIELD THAT IS FOREVER PARADISE.

THE FANS

THERE IS A CERTAIN UNIQUENESS ABOUT CELTIC FOOTBALL CLUB AND THE EMBODIMENT OF THAT COMES FROM THE FANATICAL SUPPORT WHEN 60,000 HEARTS BEAT AS ONE FAITHFULLY THROUGH AND THROUGH AND EVERY MOMENT, JOYOUS OR PAINFUL, IS SHARED AND, TO PARAPHRASE THE GREAT JOCK STEIN, "CELTIC IS NOTHING WITHOUT THE FANS."

THE PLAYERS

THEY ARE THE BHOYS WHO CARRY THE DREAMS AND ASPIRATIONS OF COUNTLESS THOUSANDS INTO EVERY SINGLE GAME WHERE EVERY SINGLE THUNDERBOLT SHOT, CRUNCHING TACKLE, LUNG BURSTING RUN AND FINGERTIP SAVE IS WATCHED WITH BATED BREATH BY THE GREEN AND WHITE FAITHFUL IN THE STANDS.

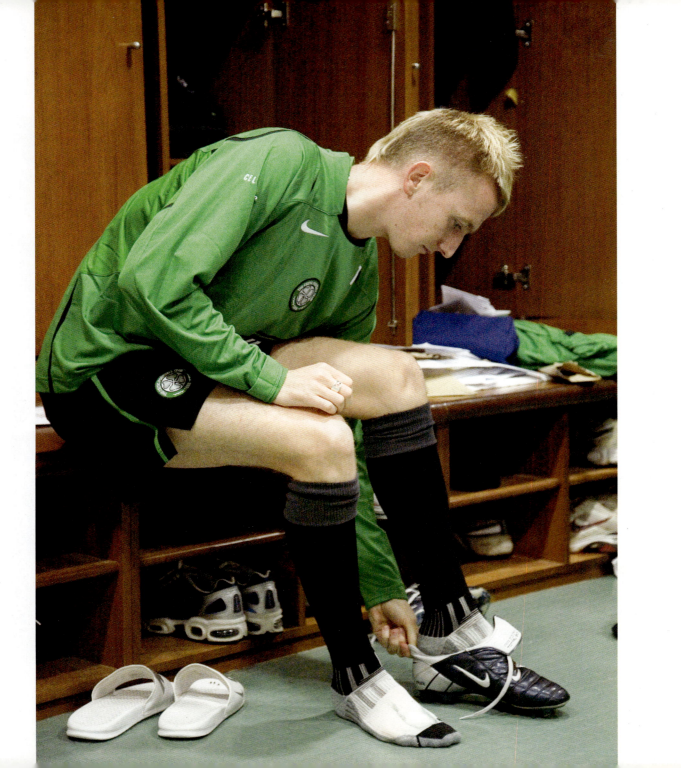

THE PREPARATION

AS LISBON LION, BERTIE AULD, ONCE FAMOUSLY QUIPPED, "WE TRAIN ALL WEEK AND ON A SATURDAY WE GET THE DAY OFF TO PLAY FOOTBALL!" TIMES MAY HAVE CHANGED FROM WHEN THE PLAYER SIMPLY LAPPED THE TRACK BUT 100 PER CENT PREPARATION GOES INTO THE BUILD UP TO EVERY CELTIC GAME AT ALL LEVELS IN THE CLUB.

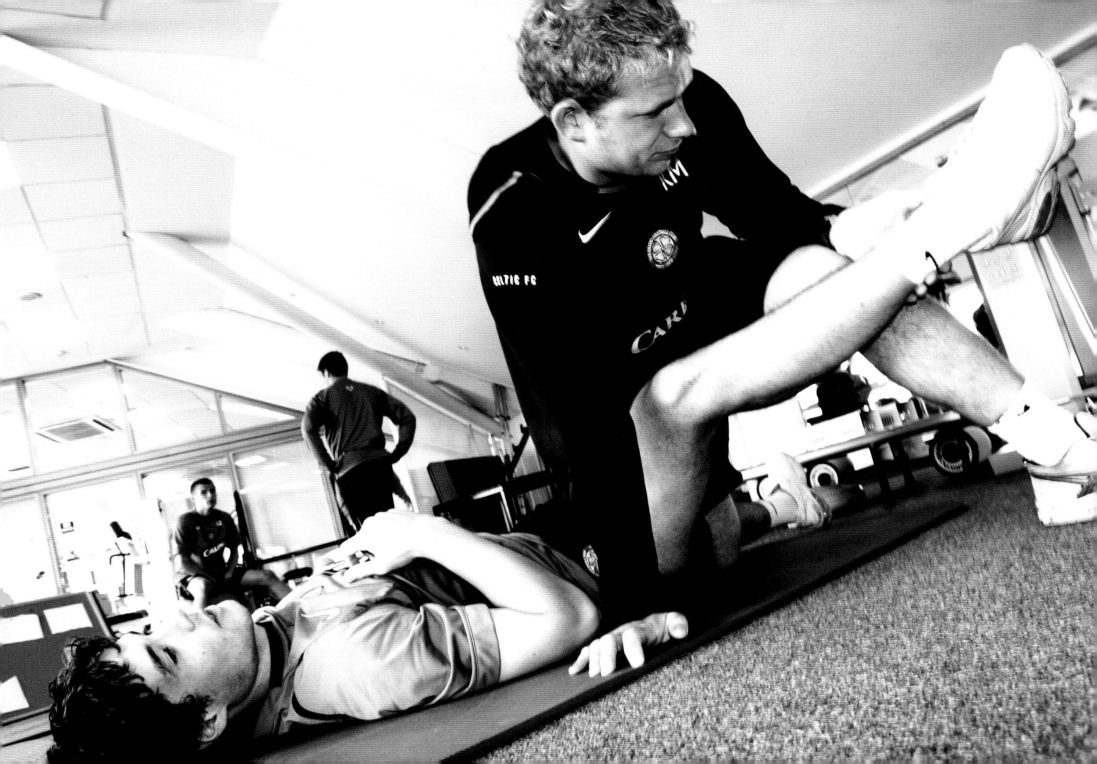

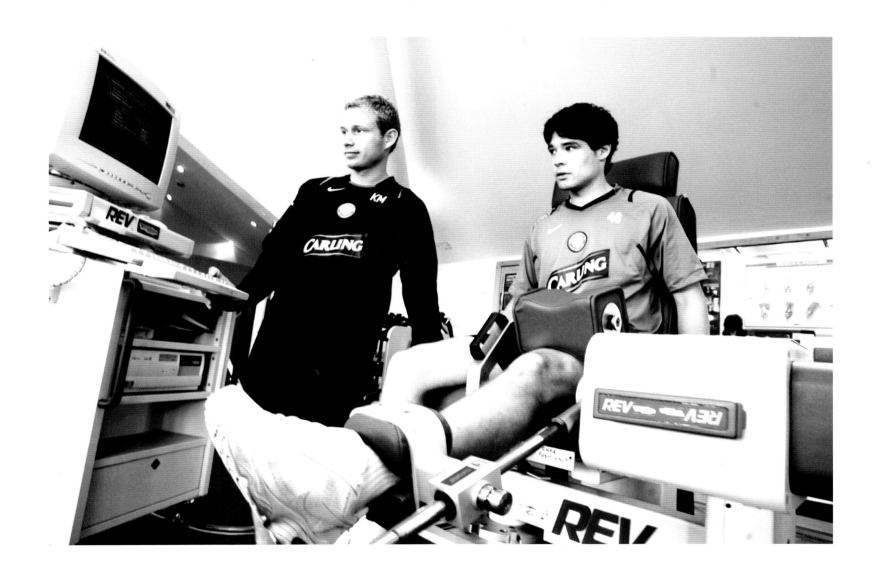

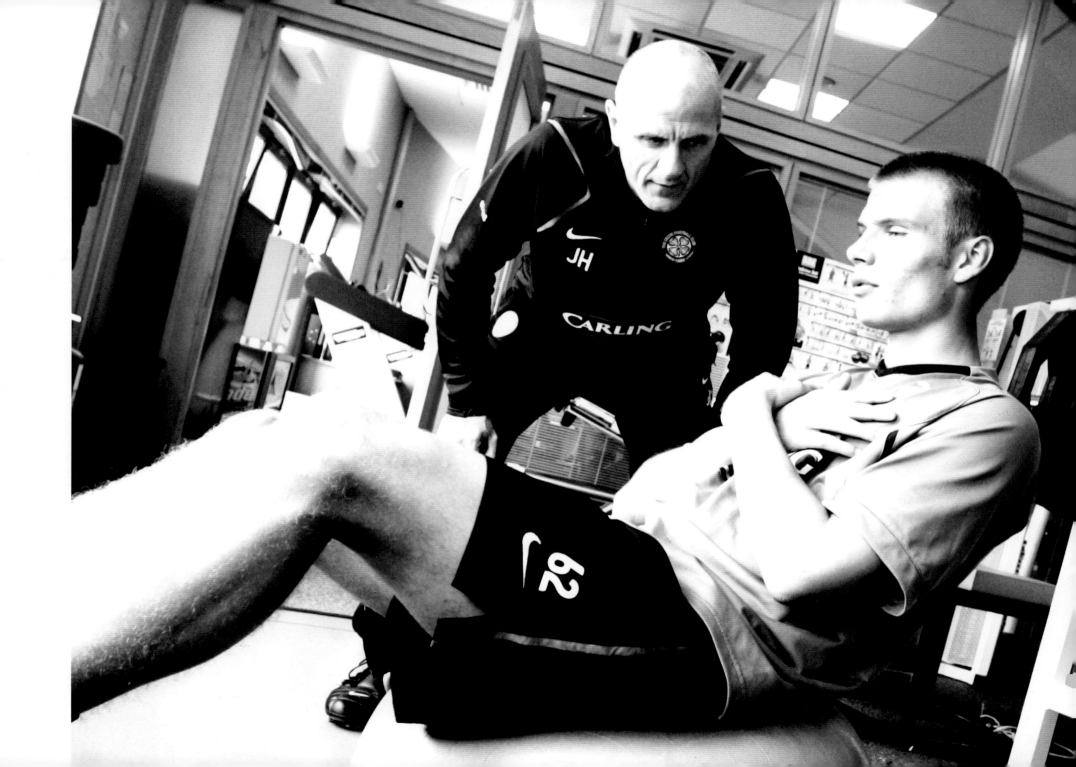

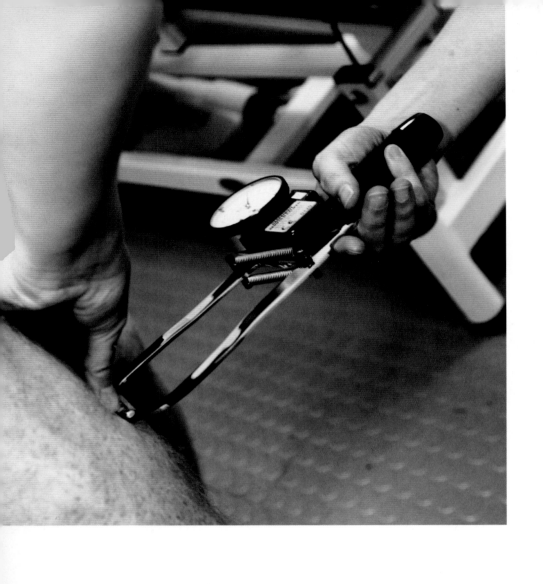

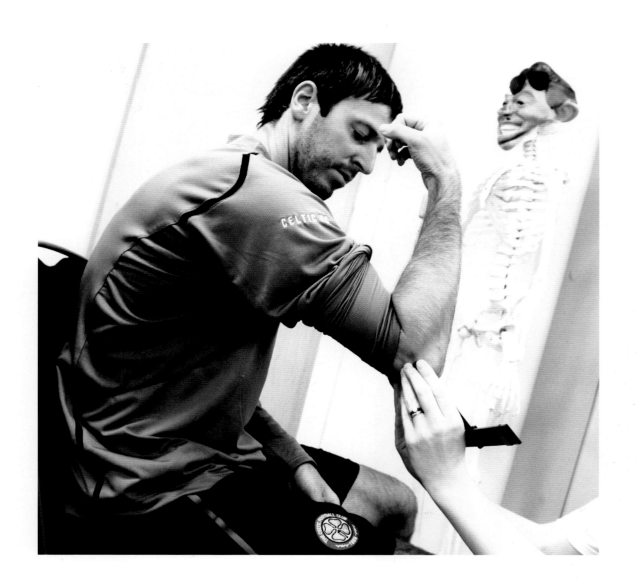

THE BUILD UP

OVER 60,000 FANS WAIT IN ANTICIPATION AS THE CELTS EMERGE FROM THE TUNNEL BUT, BEHIND THE SCENES, ONLY A LUCKY FEW PARTICIPATE IN PUTTING THE FINAL TOUCHES TO A WEEK-LONG BUILD-UP IN PREPARATION FOR THE FIRST BLOW OF THE REFEREE'S WHISTLE.

THE MATCH

IT'S A MATCHDAY AND THERE'S NOTHING QUITE LIKE IT. THE ADRENALINE IS PUMPING AND THE BUTTERFLIES RUN AMOK IN THE STOMACH AS THE TENSION RISES BEFORE KICK-OFF – AND THAT'S JUST FOR THE SUPPORTERS. BUT FOR THE PLAYERS AND FANS ALIKE, THE BEST PRESSURE VALVE IN THE WORLD IS CELEBRATING A GOAL.

THE GAFFER

IT'S SAID THAT ONCE THE PLAYERS CROSS THAT WHITE LINE ON TO THE PITCH THERE IS NOTHING MUCH THE MANAGER CAN DO! TRY TELLING THAT TO GORDON STRACHAN AS HE RUNS THROUGH THE WHOLE GAMUT OF EMOTIONS WHILE HE URGES THE PLAYERS ON TO GREATER HEIGHTS.

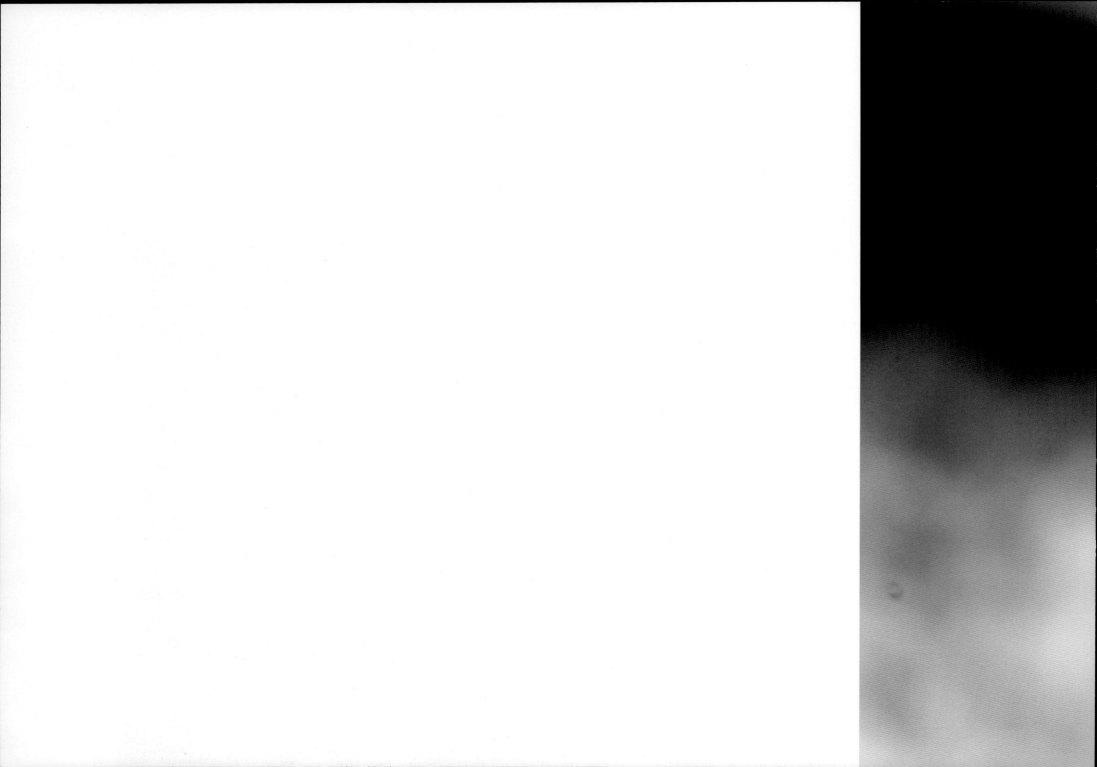

CELTIC PEOPLE

EVERYTHING CENTRES ON THE 90 MINUTES ON THE PITCH AND THE 11 MEN IN GREEN AND WHITE TAKING PART IN THE GAME – BUT CELTIC PARK IS A HIVE OF ACTIVITY 24/7 WITH HUNDREDS OF PEOPLE ENSURING EVERYTHING IS SPOT ON IN TIME FOR THE BIG KICK-OFF.

TWO LISBON LIONS REMINISCE ABOUT THE OLD DAYS AS JOHN CLARK AND BOBBY LENNOX PREPARE TO WATCH THE CURRENT CELTS IN ACTION IN ANOTHER GAME ON THEIR MARCH TOWARDS THE TITLE.

EVERYONE AT CELTIC PARK PITCHES IN AND NONE MORE SO THAN HEAD GROUNDSMAN JOHN HAYES WHO ADDED TO THE SILVERWARE AT PARADISE BY BEING THE FIRST MAN NORTH OF THE BORDER TO WIN THE PROFESSIONAL FOOTBALL GROUNDSMAN OF THE YEAR.

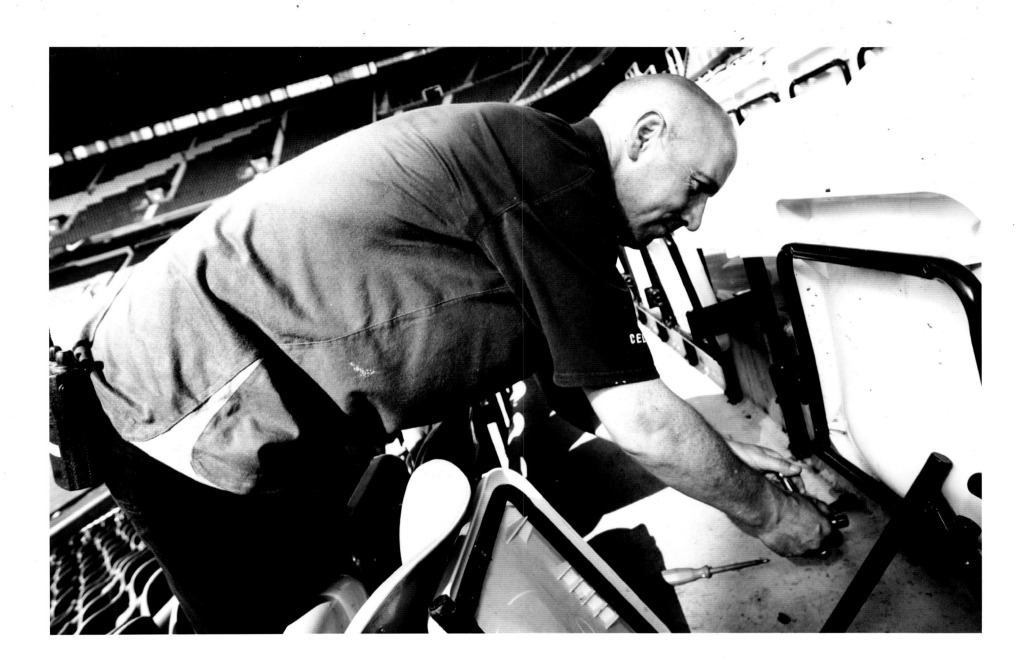